A Kind of Making

Other Books by Tom Furniss

Poetry

Play for Three Hands - co-author, 1981

Non-fiction

Edmund Burke's Aesthetic Ideology: Language, Gender and Political Economy in Revolution (Cambridge University Press, 1993, 2008)

Discovering the Footsteps of Time: Geological Travel Writing about Scotland, 1700-1820 (Edinburgh University Press, 2018, 2019)

Ways of Reading: Advanced Reading Skills for Students of English Literature - co-author (Routledge, 1992, 2000, 2007, 2012) and

Reading Poetry: An Introduction - co-author (Longman, 1996, Pearson, 2007, Routledge 2012).

Tom Furniss

A Kind of Making: Selected Poems, 1979-2018

First published in paperback format by
Coverstory books, 2019

ISBN 978-1-9993027-6-4

Copyright © Tom Furniss 2019

The right of Tom Furniss to be identified as
the author of this work has been asserted by
them in accordance with the Copyright,
Designs and Patents Act 1988.

The cover image is © Aidan Furniss, 2018.

All rights reserved.

No part of this publication may be
reproduced, circulated, stored in a system
from which it can be retrieved, or
transmitted in any form without the prior
permission in writing of the publisher.

www.coverstorybooks.com

For Jason Best, close reader and close friend for forty years.

Contents

Foreword 3

✿

Arrival in 1975 5
The Chestnut Trees are Weeping 7
Awed Beneath the Stars 8
Image 9
An Uneventful Morn 10
Hung Between Two 11
Salmon 13
We Parted Silently 14
Their Immortal Memory: The Royal Welch Fusiliers Museum in
    Caernarfon Castle 15
Crustacea 17
Apocalypse Now 18
Song of Dawn 19
Habit in the Street 21
The Chameleon 22
Break of Day 23
Corrosion: A Red-Light Poem 24
The Ceremony 26
Love Lyric 27
A Coefficient of Friction 28
Study in Black and White 29
Despedida Federico Lorca 32
Spring Sycamore 34
Bridge 35
Natural History 36
Sunrise 37
A Sepia Face 38
Windlestraw 40
A Metaphor for You 41
Crossing the Solent, 1545-1982 42
Leaving London (St Pancras Gardens) 43
Vertical Smoke 44
Dramas on a Large Scale 46
Storm 47
22 October 1983 49
At Camden Lock 55

Last Rights	57
Troping the Fields	59
Migration North	60
Dawn Breaks in the Music Room	62
Cold Higham, Winter '63	63
The Grand Union Canal	65
On St Boniface Down	66
Brook Down to Tennyson Down	68
A Turn in the Country	69
Adam's Apple	70
Christmas Eve in Heptonstall	71
Maths Questions	73
For Professor Jonathan Sawday, June 2009	74
Moving from Glasgow to Blanefield, May 2010	76
Running out of Ink at Fifty-Seven	78
For Doori: In Memoriam, 30 October 2010	79
A Conversation Poem at Nether Stowey, Summer 2011	81
A Penny Drops	86
A Ming Imperial Porcelain Flask	88
A Quiet Revolution in Blanefield, 18 September 2014	90
Souvenirs of Ivka	93
I Live on Grass	95
My Euphonium	96
Childcare in Fosters Booth	98
On Inchcolm	101
Self-Examination at 63	103
The Name Business	105
The Old Jokes Make Us Laugh	107
What Happens to a Bee with Hay Fever?	108
Hospital or Death?	110
First Apostrophe to an Invisible Embryonic Being, 16 August 2011	112
Expecting (13 December 2011)	114
Snow Baby	115
Walking with You in the Babybjörn at Eight Months Old	116
Hydrocortisone Behind my Knees	118
Cooling Fire	119
Driving to the Montessori Nursery in Killearn, July 2014	121
A Sawing Horse	123

❖

Acknowledgements	129

Foreword

I have been writing poems for nearly 50 years. My early influences – the Beatles, Dylan, Shelley, Wordsworth – are still my first loves, though I've read, taught and fallen in love with a lot of great poetry since then, from Homer to Walcott and Duffy. I wrote lots of poems before going to the University of Southampton to study English in the autumn of 1978, but they were overly romantic apprentice pieces. At university, alongside studying for my degree, I joined a writers' group led by John Birtwhistle, the writer in residence, and the critical discussion of each other's work in that group had an important impact on my writing. Three members of that group – Ian Gouge, Jason Best, and Kate Miller – were especially stimulating writers and readers. As a group, we went on to establish and edit an arts magazine, *The Definite Article*, present poetry readings, and produce a collection of our poetry, *Play for Three Hands*. Jason and I were later involved in helping Allene Tuck, also a student of English, establish and edit a literary magazine called *Between the Lines*. The experience of being an editor of other people's writing helped me to become a better editor of my own work.

The poems selected here are presented in roughly chronological order. About half of them were written in the period between 1978 and 1983, years during which I underwent intensive hot-house development that including my first degree, a year of unemployment, my MA degree, political awakening and activity, and intense loves and losses. After that time, most of my writing energy went into my PhD thesis and then into the books and articles produced during my academic career at the University of Strathclyde. Although I occasionally wrote poems in the period between 1983 and 2010, poetry returned to me in force when my wife became pregnant and when my son Aidan was born on Christmas Eve 2011. Another recent stimulant for the return to/of poetry has been writing words for songs and choral works composed by Eddie McGuire, one of Scotland's foremost classical composers and folk musicians. The title of this collection quotes from the final poem and alludes to Sir Philip Sidney's description of the poet in his *Defence of Poesie* (1595) as a 'maker'. Thanks to Aidan for the cover image, which he painted when he was seven. He said he would be proud for it to be on the cover of my book of poems. Thanks also to Jason Best and to Ian Gouge of Coverstory books.

Arrival in 1975

after ten hours at thousands of feet
riding the turbulence
you're already leaving behind
your anglo-saxon evolution,
stepping into the heat
eight thousand miles away
unsure as an off-course migratory bird
testing strange solid ground;
tired you are –
couldn't have closed eyes
to surrealist cloudscapes,
Greenland's glaciers gouging
mountains, laced with moraine,
a geography class come true,
the flat geometrical plains of Canada
growing wheat for the world,
the long Sierra range and at last
the city we'd been heading for laid out below
like a cubist woman on a canvas,
blocks of colour broken by freeways,
patches of houses where swimming pools have bred,
in affluent neighbourhoods,
like amoebas under a microscope
and downtown stood proud,
fifty stories high with people
as living and breathing as you
and then blue air filled the window
till you banked the other way
and the Pacific Ocean stretched below
flecked with the white of yachts
and Will Rogers' State Beach was a golden lace

between city and sea, flecked with golden girls;
the landing was smooth, but the customs were rough,
police guns in holsters were the first thing you saw
with your twenty-four-hours-open eyes;
the hotel room with color TV of course
was a godsend after the bus that carried you
into the palpitating heart of a city now all-too-close,
blank-faced buildings reaching for sun and air,
fall-out shelters shouldering department stores,
stations selling lead-free gas,
darkening streets teeming with all the faces
from a picture book you had as a child
that showed the faces of the world; the bus
spewed you onto the sidewalk
and you booked in fascinated by the clerk's drawl
that would soon become the accent of your thoughts;
lying in bed as the night rises and falls
with a nervous system newly adapted for flight
you stare with eyes that have lost the knack of closing
at draperies that barely shut the city out,
and thru the early hours
the movie sirens of emergency vehicles
make you feel you've arrived
not in the city of angels
but in the seventh circle of hell.

The Chestnut Trees are Weeping

What a master you are of the floodlit stage,
A kingly actor in a kingly part,
An audience subject to your merest word
As you strut and preen in royal robes
Kissing your brother's queen.

But after the curtain's dying fall
And the sound of many hands,
When the rest is silence,
And you have shuffled off
Those mortal robes of state,
You melt alone into the darkest London night
Huddled in a shapeless coat,
Unmasked,
Kissing a stale cigarette,
Yellow leaves falling around your head.

And there you stand unknown in the queue
Waiting for the midnight train.

It's easy to tell the player from the play.

Awed Beneath the Stars

I stand
              awed
beneath the cold
inhuman star-
crossed sky
              wondering
if the moon
has sunk
or is about
to rise
              watching
travellers'
headlights
cutting darkness
like a knife
through water
              drawn
to the bright-
curtained, warm-
surfaced windows
              perplexed
between
a moonrise
and a moonset
              awed
beneath the
stars.

Image

night silver
avon river
through swan quill
flowing
to touch the shores
of all nations

An Uneventful Morn

We came to a broken-down stable,
Cold and tired, and shuffled in
Among the crowd with our gifts
Of scent and gold. Ignored,
We had to elbow between
Commingled peasants and beasts,
My feet were soiled, my nose offended –
A fine welcome for wise priests!

A new-born cry, a girl laid low in straw
Haloed in the afterglow of bearing,
Naked breasts, hair matted with straw,
Needing, I thought, some privacy.

An old man stood by, bemused,
Looking to comfort, trying not to hinder,
Afraid of the large-fisted landlady
Who'd taken command,
Wrapping a red and veiny thing
To her capacious breast.

The babe screamed as if
Pierced by the nails of a world
Harsh after the womb.

My brothers bowed their heads
Even to the fouled straw ground,
And I followed suit unwilling
To seem blind, but all I could see
Was an after-birth face,
And all I could think was
That it's another poor wretch
Cast into the world, another
That women must do their best to save.

Hung Between Two

Through a broken crowd I walked
divided, towards one
whose outstretched arms
seemed eager to embrace
a whole world.

I reached my hand through
the eternal distance
between man and god to touch
his flesh
timidly
as the first touch of fingertips
of first love.

His hung head
lifted
and a murmur of pain
split the solid air.

I went to kiss those feet
but his sigh stopped my lips
and I looked, afraid,
into his face
and his eyes warmed and burned
with all the mystery of fire.

Hung between a tear
and a smile
he shook his thorned head
and I knew his blessing
and his farewell.

I left hung
between sorrow and joy
knowing his outstretched arms
were nailed to the cross forever
                                      for me.

Salmon

heavy with instinct
salmon cram river mouths
a mass idea
carrying each against the flow

fished
by otters net-men weakness fate,
the fittest survive,
in glass-bead eyes instinct
hardens into purpose

leaping at waterfalls
scraping soft flanks
across rocks
the urge to relax
float downstream clamours
like a devil in the mind

red and bloated and alone
they nuzzle holes in calm pools
spawn life from dying bodies
make it safe in the sand
with a spasm of the tail

and then let go

We Parted Silently

walking you down to the station
I hands in pockets you bright in the sun
we searching for rationalisation

let's face it, it just wasn't working
standing at the turnstile eyes averting
then silence waiting what is she wondering

aware of the clock ten minutes to go
but this ended long since the time goes slow
but neither wants another minute and both know

your attempt to smile stuck in my thought
and that last closed kiss when no tongue sought
to explore or explain or make bitter retort

Their Immortal Memory: The Royal Welch Fusiliers Museum in Caernarfon Castle

Just a series of fading faces,
Photographs maybe
Of old-men's half-forgotten brothers,
Long dead mothers' sons,
Peaked caps and earth-coloured uniforms
Of World War I,
Pallid faces with eyes
Fixed and bewildered
By the still-new-fangled device
Taking something of their lives.

Faces with a common shadow cast
Over little-lost-boyness,
Upright, very upright
With manly brave moustaches,
Caps tilted at cocky angles
And hard-to-bear smiles,
Perhaps having written first and last
Homesick letters home.

Fresh-faced from hymns and hills
Aged in the plains of Amiens,
Eyes hollowed out
By staring after death in the night.

Sepia heroes,
Victoria Crosses to bear,
Forced into halls of fame,
They achieved a kind of manhood
Briefly before death.

Accounts of deeds
Are tagged to frames
Telling brave tales
But eyes speak more tellingly.

A little boy stares me in the eye
A bugler or drummer
In a proud uniform – so young
To be so crossed.

Heroic for the flag
The bright and brave music
And the old commandments
Scapegoats following a goat
To slaughter
Falling for the glory
Of the regiment whose history
Is honoured in a castle built
Seven hundred years ago
To put down Welsh rebellions.

Leaving the museum to its memories,
A ragged and dirty rectangle
Of once-coloured canvass
Hoverers above my head,
Something to die for.

Crustacea

in the living room
the to-and-fro of tides
and the shifting of sands
was in our conversation

nothing settled that night
no tidings for a drift-wood world
only admiration
for the solutions of evolution
exoskeletons for animals
lacking backbones
and the example of a hermit crab
caught exposed now and then
between shells – only to scuttle
into the nearest empty remains
of a common whelk
at the first awareness of us

but then the seeing of it
the trace along the sand
will stay till a storm

Apocalypse Now

in a breathing sweating chaos
spontaneous fission and fusion and their consequent
sudden spill of energy, reserved scholars
made passes at startled girls, embrace of lovers
found envious focal points in pairs
of lonely eyes, though their own vision
microscopically sought and found nothing
but themselves enlarged

awesome power bonds proton to neutron yet
bonds break under the savage pressures
at the solar heart – a final split you'd think
would rend a nucleus in a nova blaze
that no one could miss

when their time has come stars
collapse into themselves,
generate all the elements
to build a universe
or black holes from which,
until recently we thought,
there is no escape

only rare souls break out
of orbits finely poised
between gravity and momentum,
achieve escape velocity,
and fewer still give shoulder to another –
a still small place somewhere in the storm
of an imploding universe

Song of Dawn

bird of dawning
sing night away
cabaret the nightmare
of all-too-human flesh
on crooked cross,
shoulder it, siren
the stranger
wandering for an island in the flood,
the seafarer dove,
look to eastward
fish for timid sun
even to burn of feathers
smell of burnt bone

I seek for a stone to stay my wings
wet with salt and wandering

throw me a throwaway line,
even a gethsemane kiss
would be a touch of lips
wet of your breath
would be something of you extending
across the great shoulders of hills
that between us must lie

smear of death on life
red of a moment's fatality
black of ceremonious sorrow
green of forgotten grave

mortal gull wheel in blood sky
sweet sad gesture of deferral
defying the final crunch of bone on stone
tight sinews pulling against the lure
of earth, overlooking green
of mould-tipped feather
first colour of decay

countless feet find footing
on an earth ribbed with bones

Habit in the Street

a black coif cascades down your back
ripples as you walk
waves as the wind plays
fails to veil the motion of your hair

a gleam of gilt rings your finger
a band of gold fencing out,
enclosing in, you from me,
with the pride of a ringed bird, bride of Christ

your habit thwarts not mine

The Chameleon

The chameleon
                     lies
Green among green blades
Made known to me only
By its shadow

Self portrait painter
Can you tell the painter from the paint
Painting landscapes from a mirror

Is yours a chameleon universe
Seen through chameleon eyes

Blank canvas
                     lies
And awaits discoloration

Blades landscape flesh

Canvas-coloured brush colours canvas
With a self-re-veiling blush

The chameleon
                     lies

Break of Day

Children's feet break
The crust of morning snow
As the head of Christ broke
The Virgin

Tamed by hunger to feed
On broken bread
Scraps of last night's supper
A robin like blood
Spilt in the garden
Makes its mark
But leaves no stain
As nails
On the risen day

Corrosion: A Red-Light Poem

the corrosion of scaffolding
against an ancient monument
metal exoskeleton
making the church stand still

keeping up the public face
against the oldest profession
members of the council stand still
against a fallen girl's doorway

scaffolding leaning or being
leaned upon by house or home
bricks and mortar or hearth fire
glowing or reflecting the sun's

russet gleam, brindled bricks
of deceptive fire, windows lit
at just the angle for the retina
just the colour of the blood

the home-making-or-breaking fire
flushing faces out
late into the night
roving streets ringing doorbells

A church leans
From what it means
To what it knows
Doubt grows

As to the architect
And the effect
Of building on clay
Bells play

By their iron heart
A heavy part
When heavy bells are rung
An iron tongue

With metallic tone
Will shake soft stone
And scaffolding
Will itself swing

The Ceremony

deaf stone
enclosing expired air
condensation running in beads
on the walls, the inside walls

a few high windows
stained to stop the eye

dead expressions
intended to light up faces
a devoted holding of the body
chilling the blood

and at the sacred heart
a ceremony
celebrating union
a relic of wine
and softening wafers

ringing marble

a ring to bind till death
a closed circle
stone death

Love Lyric

and you and I
may either die
tomorrow
laying flowers
on the earth
or if it is not to be
we will cut
each other's flower
and lie
each with each
in the earth

A Coefficient of Friction

ringlets of bright steel
tangled and burnt blue –
a coefficient of friction –
by the song of machines built
on revolutionary principles

dull ingots of raw steel
turned into machine parts
leaving pared-away ringlets
like unmanageable curls
to be swept from the factory floor
thrown on the scrap heap
as material for the song
of revolutionary poets

STUDY IN BLACK AND WHITE

the gentle eye
shot aspirations
of the spired city

APPLICANTS ARE FILTERED

a film of oil
smooths a river
broken by dip of oar

stone cut of Cotswolds
seems grey
in the monochrome

A QUESTION OF BACKGROUND

a girl's progress
balanced on a bicycle
at eighteen

the half-tone features
of her half-child face
over-exposed and under-developed

ADMISSIONS PROCEDURE

rare botanical gardens
by a river frozen
in one 500th of a second

and you
walking out of the picture
before I could measure the light

NO ENTRANCE

in the park deer study
the eye of the lens
through iron railings

turn to the ritual of rutting
fast locked together
by the flick of a shutter

WITHOUT AUTHORITY

the camera peers
through a spired fence
at Magdalene Collage

to snap
reverently
its fading image

UNLESS ACCOMPANIED

a background of composed gardens
that yet might bear the imprint
of poet or painter

framed by the sharply focussed fence –
with an infinite depth of field
a camera misses nothing

BY A BADGED MEMBER OF THE COLLEGE

outside the frame
workmen in the street study
work in progress

and she
developing into a love
has cycled by

Despedida Federico Lorca

(after seeing Ballet Rambert's performance of *Cruel Garden* at Southampton's Gaumont Theatre in 1981)

1.
like a girl with a veil
drawing and withdrawing
the crowded eyes
                      open
for a spectacle
an initiation
by the bloodshot head of a bull

like a coquette he plays
Olé!
to delight their eyes

but horns tear satin flesh
thrill of blood petals the hot earth

clutched to a mother
staining her veil
a craftsman of the ring gored
in pursuit
of an absolute purity of line

2.
slogans are painted in blood
on the walls of the ring
on the city walls
on the frontier fences

a poet returns from exile
as an orphan to a mother
mourning all her sons

red petals strew the streets
where a child played el matador
in love with the idea
of the fight, fighting
the idea of love

ideas have stained since then

brutality is beauty
weddings are sheddings of blood

El Cafe de Chintas
rings with the cadence of decay

a black-headed bull
tosses frenziedly
the shreds of a veil

red petals curl in the sun

the ring is silent

despedida, Federico

Spring Sycamore

imbibes from its watershed
nutriments dissolved in the shed water
of a crown spread twenty feet
absorbed in fine as hair capillaries
sucked from the catchment area of a circle
π times ten feet squared
the impossible miracle of life
consummated in the capillary surge
of budding desire
elevating nurture
to its upper & outermost ends
where life is eternally beginning
out of the corpse of wood
that supports & strengthens against
worm and storm its limbs even to a spread
of twenty feet & bursts buds
grasping at the sky open
like lungs gasping air
bursting buds into burdens
bowing with birds to spring

Bridge

I shuffle, cut, deal to myself
dividing the pack into four
one hand pretending not to know
what the other is doing
imagining you across the table
responding

we always play the hand going for game
overbidding in the first
but taking the rubber
with a small slam in hearts

before you partnered me
imagination was enough
now I cannot live by thinking alone

I write a poem
in a bid for your response
not knowing how many points I hold

I wait for your call

Natural History

in the beginning
a smooth perfect curve of shell
a batch of white against
the colour of decay

then a tremor
like the earth quaking
a crack
like a sudden fault
in an earthenware bowl
a forked tongue already flickering
for flesh
a smooth penis head
with a long scaled body
like a train of consequences uncoiling
from a cramped womb
sloughing off the warmth of decomposing matter
that has brooded over the bearing
of this subtle death-bringing beast

one more harmless grass-snake slithers away

Sunrise

you open eyes
a sunrise
upon chiselled hills
of shoulders, thighs
and dew of morning skies

you free the stone-trapped man
articulating limbs and can
discover in me so lovingly
before the world began
the beginnings of a man

your ultra-violet eyes play
on me the sleeping clay
firing earthen form
the photosynthetic way
offering me to dawning day

in all my naked prime

A Sepia Face

A sepia face next to an old clock
That measured an afternoon's sleepy pace,
A sepia mouth and eyes like my mother's
But with shorter hair like a boy's.

The way the figure faded into white,
The main features barely seeming to have brushed
The paper, like an old brown watercolour,
Seemed to me like her fate.

She'd played a long time ago with my mother
Who was Lily then and a little girl,
Barely as old as I. But Joyce,
A little the elder, my grandmother said,

Each time I took the frame from the side,
Had gone away somewhere to wait for us
Because of something called polio from swimming.
I wonder, as I visualise that face,

If that's where I caught my fear
Of water. The grave
Had never been marked by a stone
And a generation of winters had thawed

And seeped away till none could remember
Exactly which mound it was. And though
They often talked of mounding it again
And buying a stone, it was never done –

Somehow the thought of honouring another's grave
By mistake, and neglecting hers,
Made even the annual trimming in the spring,
And the placing of flowers, an uncertain ceremony.

The old clock stopped
When the fingers that wound it grew stiff.
The sepia face – the only memento
I'd have liked – was burnt with the rest.

Windlestraw

windlestraw, an ash-blonde's unpinned hair,
loosened for the wind to play,
lit by the scattered shards
of the Itchen, leaning

over the troubled meniscus, a brow
furrowed with runnels of light,
to still, with the merest touch of wand,
incoherent images, clutching

at the wind-troubled waves
to pin them carefully into place

A Metaphor for You

writing these letters
to span the space
between now and then, between
here and there

toiled over this,
sleet brushing the street,
to form, between slush and ice,
a single crystal of snow

all I can say is sorry
for things I omit and things I do,
distance may be necessary for metaphor
but I'd rather have you –

because snow won't do
as a metaphor
it's far too cold
for you

Crossing the Solent, 1545-1982

hardly out of port
and drowned like a rat,
though no actual rats could be found,
capsized, it's often said,
before the safety margin made design a science,
by the weight of guns that were
to have sunk the French –
drowned in these perilous seas
where concrete forts would be built,
three centuries on, to guard
against the same invader – drowned
a dozen fathoms below the wake
of this regular ferry to Ryde,
a rude berth for those
press-ganged to a death
that still catches at the breath
with the force of a familiar nightmare
as I search for the security
of boats and belts strapped to a hull
that could never sink, rehearsing a TV scene
of the SOS technology of the Coast Guard.

I saw the largest crane in the world
wading the Solent, carefully angling
for the fragile Mary Rose,
and more recently, the catch
having been suitably framed,
an American woman on TV South
who'd paid a thousand pounds to step on board.

Leaving London (St Pancras Gardens)

Leaves spun from London trees
spin you to catch at luck, you said,
before it spills to the ground,
the first hand ever to touch
its fine-spun web, bruising
its already-decaying weave
as fingers close. I catch
an echo of childhood and cannot
take the wafer from your hand,
and will not spin for one myself.
Nor can we give one to the man
who sits and stares from the park bench
facing nothing, nothing in his face, while
leaves spin around his head,
catch at his hair, spill to the ground.
Childhood was as delusive as its rites.
The sacks of leaves I collected
to pad the arms and legs of Guy Fawkes
year after year, re-limbed something
that never was, put to the fire
that which never went to the fire.
Leaves of autobiography burn
as they spill from the pen.
A man wheels a barrow into the park
and takes a stiff brush to the leaves,
beginning to clear the leaves from London.
A lot will depend on that barrow.

Vertical Smoke

Vertical smoke
of suburban fires supplements
a landscape frore as March can make it
this far south. No wind
no scent of danger disturbs
this stay-in-bed Sunday.

We set out for an excursion undeterred
by the yet-to-be-broken ice spanning
Range Rover tracks impressed
on softer days in earth not meant for us.
'Private Property' means what it says,
the stress falling on alliteration
and none at all on implication.

Gulls score intersecting circles
in the wake of ploughing blades, as if
the worms were turned for them,
and they in turn for us. The farmer works
while the population left behind sleeps
late into the day of rest. The daughters
of eccentric old gentlemen exercise
horses. Young thighs domineer
expensive mounts. You and I
talk of revolution yet keep
to the Ordinance Survey route.
Possession is all of the law.

Lifting ourselves step by step beyond
these sea-level atmospherics
to the tumuli that mark an older order,
the still undisturbed air troubles
your brow, as if rearranging your thoughts
about peace and what it might mean to breach
that of the lieges.

Descending towards vertical smoke
we talk inevitably of politics
and of when the wind blows.

Dramas on a Large Scale

The enormous tragedy of the dream
in the peasant's bent shoulders, bent
on weaving, or perhaps knitting,
plain and pearl, plain and pearl, the
enormous fields of earth, aroused
like that of a couple well into marriage
as the planet's orientation turns
toward spring, the ritual of the ploughshare
crossing and re-crossing the wide space, folding
the winter-softened stubble into the earth, gradually
turning the field's new face to the sky.

First it was the snowdrops in the snow
that old cliché again and then
egg-yolk crocuses breaking out from monochrome,
the ever-new shock of daffodils,
and lengthening days stretching
my body once again on a sensual rack
as girls shed winter clothes like buds bursting
from dead wood – the casual comedy
of perennial desire in suburban gardens.

Storm

in the briefest of lulls
in this hottest of summers,
night kept back with curtains
and with flare of tungsten,
rhythms of rain strange on the ear
beyond the window slats
glistening with the distance nostalgia brings
to sounds of other human beings
living other lives, pausing
between noun and adjective,
stretching embrowned limbs
to push tangible solitude
towards its limit, turn to pen the storm,
blowing woodwind and reeds,
approaching the ear –
a seed parachutes through the slats
as if for refuge, falls
on the book of definitions
with all the pathos of blind faith
as the storm swells the currents of air
forced over a reed tautened
to an almost erotic sensitivity to touch,
swelling towards a scream
that rattles the slats and drowns
all human sounds,
pounding leaves to sound like cymbals
as peals of thunder impose the rhythm
of the mad march towards a midnight
prophesised in every poem up to this moment
bending time to a beat
that raises the pace, shortens

the intervals as the storm's core accelerates
towards this shrinking solitude
till the lightning seems to come inside the head
curling limbs back to a foetal whorl
under the fragile coverlid that barely filters
these childish imitations of human speech
pitched at the intensity of screams
that seem to splutter from the breast
like unwanted memories
which a desperate turn to the passage
of words over paper, storm-blown ink,
in search of that still small place
before the words broke loose letting
the storm lash in through rattling slats,
will not stem nor turn to arbitrary signs –
turn the TV which way you will
it's nothing but reports of the storm
and warnings to pull out the plug …

the night now is almost tender
the dying scents of a few last sprays
of honeysuckle barely stir
a floral curtain open to the dusk,
a charm falls from its clasp,
a dress from burnished shoulders,
and early apples, beaten by the storm,
fall one by one from trees.

22 October 1983

I.

nuclear bombs kill Tories too
doo dah, doo dah
nuclear bombs kill policemen too
oh doo dah dey ...

half a million march through the capital
the sun unusually bright
for London in the fall

we hardly knew ourselves that day
or knew the city

but a shadow fell over the crowd flowing
through the streets of Whitehall
fell from inscrutable masonry of power:
solid doors of the Ministry of Defence,
a deserted Downing Street fenced with blue,
the Cenotaph for which
each one of us was a wreath pinned with poppies

where will any of us be a year from now

two four six eight
we don't want to radiate

sunset for CND sang the Sunday Times
conspiring with Scotland Yard,
its first edition which appeared about noon said
one hundred and fifty thousand
had attended a rally –
we read it still crossing the London bridges
joking with the vendors

there's no news but the old news
in these premature times ...

Maggie Maggie Maggie
Out Out Out

in the park the grass was still warm
from the long hot summer
and I half expected the Stones to be there
like the summer of '69,
but it was quieter than that, and more intense
and though there was carnival, summer had waned:
The Guardian told us that troops were standing by
for the Greenham missile date

the crowd at sunset called
for speech! speech! as Michael Foot
cradled the dog and waved the stick
that have become symbols in our time

that last wave rippled through the serried ranks
like wind through grass
as if a mirror had been shattered
into half a million

walking from the park,
the sun cremating itself in the Serpentine
before the horizon buried it,
the still-playing children's faces
fading into dusk, blank cut-outs gyrating
in the fusing light, we were still singing
the old Joan Baez song
that we might overcome

half a million marched in the capital
two men in Geneva walk in the woods

II.

thousands of ordinary women
breach the peace to give peace a chance
linking arms to refuse Cruise, embracing the base
only for it to recoil itself
behind the iron curtain of its own design

this is a common cause
an act of enclosure that curtails
a way of life, devastates
a landscape

the fence is pinned
with arms and legs of dolls,
photographs of children, and written notes
that seem to have blown from an outside world
whose messages could never cross
a dividing line designed
to keep the women out and the men in

women breaking down the fence
are liable to be shot as terrorists,
much as they shot deserters and objectors
in the '14-'18 war

ten green soldiers standing on the base
ten green soldiers standing on the base
but if one green soldier
should accidentally think …

the sun falls on a candle-lit vigil
reclaiming the night

the Yanks are coming
the Yanks are coming,
over here, over here,

they can do Europe in less than an hour now,
spread the word, spread the word

two four six eight
ten nine eight seven

III.

a Pembrokeshire sun explodes
on the Gulf Stream finally beaching
in this cove,
my running feet break
the lone and level sand,
police escort the American way of life
up the long A34,
a US Starfighter gently lays
its cuckoo eggs in the nest

Cruise is Here blazed the Sun
dawn of an era,
Cruise is Here echoed the Express

the shock of the headline
hits me on this remote coast
breaking a lyric interlude

returning to the country of the crime
by pre-nuclear British Rail
nothing fundamental seems to have changed

opposite me in the carriage
a man holds a copy of the Sun
to veil himself from me
intently reading Wyndham Lewis

a face peeks from behind the tabloid,
initiates hostilities with a smile,

withdraws again and speaks behind the pages
to the girl, a stranger, to his left,
makes, so that I cannot hear
but know myself the butt,
a joke at his own expense

she, in sympathy with me,
against her better feelings has to laugh –
the ally becomes a victim too

he, one of the moral majority,
illuminated by the Sun, too easily arouses
retaliation in my blood –
no dual key to me in a state of red alert

the cold war is maintained on both sides
through the heart of southern England
and I could even concur with Tarr
that the people need some kind of blast
to wake them from the dead, and cannot –
priming myself for mutually assured destruction –
see him as a victim of that rhetoric
he reads for truth

but at the eleventh hour this poem intervenes,
reveals to me my own complicity
in that which I protest against

we are fools to bisect the circle
of this earth, to invest east and west disjointedly
with power over our very atoms

the wind will blow through the hawthorns
but will not chill those
who walk in the woods with our fate in their hands

'tis the time's plague when madmen lead the blind

remember remember the 5th of November
plutonium treason and plot
I see no reason why Parliament's treason
should ever be forgot

for that's the way the world will end

IV.

on Hiroshima Day when the sun had sunk
hundreds of paper boats were launched
on the Itchen with candles in the wind;
they were meant as symbols of those
whose deaths might well prefigure our own
and were to have drifted out to the Solent
where I imagined them crossing the seas
to all the corners of the earth,
but they foundered less than a hundred yards
from the hands that launched,
candles snuffed in the relatively tidal wave

remember remember ...

while I deliberate
about the placing of these words
the Greenham Common women
argue points of law
with the Supreme High Court in Washington
and face another winter in the woods

I wait for a knock on the door –
I saw the Special Branch filming the march

six five four three
the sun is counting down ...

At Camden Lock

strolling in Camden Town
I come to the lock that unseals
and seals the Regent's Canal,
nostalgically pace the towpath towards King's Cross
but only a step or two –
there's nothing for me now
along that ancient cut between
the boroughs, once a thoroughfare
for you and I, a narrow strip
of an old industrial England remote enough
from the fray of the Caledonian Road,
overhung by gasometers, reflecting
cranes arranging girders
right up to its banks,
sealed off at each of its bridges
with corrugated iron which you limboed under
and I slid round, locks and quays
buoyant with winter ducks breasting
through surface scum, heavy with barges
dredging a route Irish navvies dug
spade by spade, linking your Kings Cross flat
with Compendium Books for me
and the second-hand clothes emporium for you

but now as I sort through old exotic clothes
knowing the ones you'd like
each lock is closed for me
and the corrugations cannot be passed
and the bridges can only be crossed and not gone through,
and I cannot tread that path or run my hand
where horses' chains grooved iron stanchions;

and though I still have the key to your door,
less than a mile from here,
and a series of black and white photographs –
barges under bridges, light through tunnels,
drops of lucent water breaking dark meniscus
like beads of mercury, your face lit
by tremulous reflections –
you are unreachable as yesterday.

Last Rights

steel sleet,
a sodden beauty in the chartered streets,
a sudden march in the season –
death's aflame in the yellow leaves'
last break from the prison of trees
caught up in the late rain's gutterwash

men in florescent yellow sweep
the street and branches bare
of leaves that would haunt the wind that sweeps
the earth in vain as darkness strips
day of its last light –
as if the trees would never bud again
and winter were the last of the seasons

in Trafalgar Square
under Nelson's stare and the flare
of floodlights, night
falls on the fall of man,
a pistol shot of fireworks scatters
pigeons from the silly heads
of Landseer's lions

the Reverend Jessie Jackson's single amplified voice
braves the horror of a London closing in,
sputters and cracks
from embassy to embassy, the wind tearing
and tearing at the flags, ignites
one hundred thousand faces
yellow and black and pale and hectic red

men in the blue of the force sweep
into the square trampling and truncheoning
the multitude, would strip that voice from the air –
as if it weren't already broadcast,
as if spring weren't already
working to burst that seed into flame.

Troping the Fields

turning the earth of my father's plot I say
the words I heard his father say in turn
tilling the plot they sold at his death,
his eyes blind to the flush of my face

turning ploughshares into words and words
into ploughshares I thought of a distant cousin
of mine who'd died in the field, shot
as day shot the night to shreds

we plough the field and scatter good seed,
we tilled the fields of Flanders
with our words of till we meet again,
those who live by the word, sometimes die for it

because I hope to turn once more
to the soil before I die, to find
a lost inheritance before the dust to dust,
I'll be turning in my grave when you write my epitaph

Migration North

it's a moving business,
the next best stressful thing
to losing a loved one,
it's also a question of transport, ecstasy,
and I am beside myself beside
belongings that have long been part of me
but no longer seem to fit, all boxed up
and all too tangible

packing is forcing books in boxes
not made for them, disordering
a lifetime's reading according
to the dimensions of Domestos
and Typhoo Tea

is juggling thirty years' souvenirs –
every picture's story, every
record's sleeve, every postcard's sender,
packed into these last few hours,
a lifetime passing before my eyes

moving is taking the jumble of a past
normally kept in drawers, on shelves,
under lock and key, touching
it all and having it touch me,
is adding it all up and feeling
the weight of it, afraid
it might not fit together again, or might be lost
between here and there

at these moments, the urge to shed it all
and step on some other continent
that has no past, carried
like a mayflower on a storm, dropping
an old life like a butterfly, then
when it lies so heavily on the back
and in the hand, when it stands
so solidly for the past

yet paper and vinyl and china metaphors
hold against the stress between then and now,
take the strain between here and there,
still moving me as I move them,
all packed up into moving words

Dawn Breaks in the Music Room

frost fronds the window
her fingers freeze
on minor keys

slowly Sunday morning melts
peals of bells
into hard air

beats across fields
from shire to shire
from spire to spire

runs down holy brickwork
into graves
evaporates like souls

slowly bone releases itself
from ivory, fingers
tune themselves from key to key

Cold Higham, Winter '63

I was in primary school back then
a hundred yards along the Banbury Lane
from the council house that was the centre of my world
until 1965,
the year of *Help!*
and the only holiday we ever had –
I used to measure out my life in Beatles' songs,
knew all the words and dates:
'I Want to Hold Your Hand'
in the winter of '63,
the hardest longest winter
since '47, a months'-long frost-hardened
snow-filled sledging-weather winter
when iron-hard snowdrifts allowed us to tramp
over well-known hedges so deeply buried
you'd never know they were there

we kept a singing bird in a cage
hanging in the window where it played
with its toys above the kitchen sink
in which we used to sit
one after the other
to be scrubbed from head to toe
listening to the mellow tones of the BBC
on an old valve radio
on which I heard 'Please Please Me'
oh yeah like I please you
for the first time in my life

one morning
after a frost still harder than ever
the kitchen was silent
the high-strung bell hung motionless,
the tiny mirror safe from beak attack
and the empty perch was still

the kitchen was warmed by a back oven
but only when the fire was lit
and only slowly then
and when I came home from school
the bird was laying on the black iron range,
a futile attempt at resurrection

I don't know what my parents did
with that tiny balsa-wood body,
the ground in my corner of the garden
where a lilac bloomed in summer
over the graves of all the stiff cold creatures
that I found in fields and woods
was frozen too hard for digging

The Grand Union Canal

two fishermen, middle aged,
sit on the tow-path
of the Grand Union Canal
just far enough apart not to get entangled
but near enough for manly talk

I think of the navvies who dug this cut
spade by spade from London
all the way to Birmingham
at a pace that must have seemed
more slow and hazardous than
the storm-beat crossing to the New World
that thousands of Irish made
who would not spade the English earth

this is where I learned to fish
for roach and perch with rod and line
and watched houseboats and barges
plying back and forth towing their wash;
one day I saw a bore like a tidal wave
race from north to south, thought
long and hard on what it meant

there were no fishermen, no navvies,
no barge-men to ask; luckily,
I was alone.

On St Boniface Down

from the ancient barrow
on the highest point on the Isle of Wight,
I can see the village of Bonchurch,
taking its name from the saint
who, 1200 years ago,
if the story is true,
stood right here

first settled in prehistory,
and then by Stone Age men
and then by Romans,
all drinking from the sacred spring,
a place where celebrated writers
came and lived and died,
and constellations woke
the sleeping singer from his atheist grave,
and a battle was fought to keep out the French

I watch the ferries heading for France,
a pure silver line between sea and sky,
and think of those children of France
we taught English and grew to love
in a house down there where Dickens stayed and wrote

I didn't find the wishing well
but took a path to Bonchurch Landslips
through the Devil's Chimney
and thought of those hot weeks we spent
together here in the summer-time
of our love and made my way
to Luccombe Chine where once we swam

so naked in the arms of the sea
under the holm oak undercliff

That was half a lifetime ago,
but I'd give it all gladly
if our lives had stayed like that;
I wish I wish I wish in vain,
but I'll try to find
that wishing well again.

Brook Down to Tennyson Down

Five barrows and tumuli crown
Brook Down, intervals
of sun set alight the wind
as it ripples fields of oats like the sea
and illuminate the green sand
that shelves into the sea to the east
and the white of the chalk
that south-westerlies have torn
from the cliffs of Tennyson Down
and plunged in the eager sea,
the sun-lit gale grips the gulls,
clears out the last traces of city air
from lungs that expand with prehistoric life
of tumuli men who knew the crests
that overlook the lie of the land
where enemies or friends might march and felt
a meaning that was more than self-defence;
this is my solstice festival as the wind
fills my ears with a vitality that
is close to pain and my eyes
again and again
follow the curve of Tennyson's trail
as it sweeps the huge chalk back
of the island and leads to its exposure
by and to the sea, eyes grow dim with
salt-bitten wind and the film of the past,
my umbrella becomes a spear,
my posture against the wind rooted
in race and cult

A Turn in the Country

clutching a slim volume of verse
and a slim waist, the whole world
in his hands, a poet
takes a turn in the country
for a metaphor or two,
twists flowers into a chain,
opens leaves for all they might contain
and gives them to the wind,
an eye at work on a figure
in the hidden folds of fields
hardly lingering over the letter of the law,
taking hold of whatever comes to hand,
buds bursting under fingers
that caress and trope the world
to other ends than those allowed
by the law of letters

Adam's Apple

Adam's apple stuck
in his throat
and he found himself talking
in a lower note

Eve it seems
swallowed it whole
coming from a honeyed tongue
straight to her soul

the birds and the bees
all flew for cover
when Adam rebuked Eve
in the tone of a lover

Eve's reply
is not recorded
she just did what
her god had ordered

what she replied
we are not told,
she just did what
her god foretold

Christmas Eve in Heptonstall

high above Hebden Bridge
clinging to the side of the Calder Valley
a rookery in bare oaks
an eagle couched on cliff-face
remains of early industry worn down
by wilderness and loss
a place for northern poetry

walking in Hardcastle Wood,
shades of Elmet on the moor
a mist folds and parts
light drains from the air, dark condenses
into ghosts of stone

every stone in this stone village
was cut by hand, hauled up
this inclination, one in seven,
then raised one by one still higher
guided into line by a builder's plumb

mills and chapels erode
the carcass of a church, burnt ribs arching
above hammer horror headstones
treacherous to tread, and a legend of you
standing in black under arches
caught in photograph and poem
and in my brain

black village of gravestones
skull of an idiot
whose dreams die back
where they were born

skull of a sheep
whose meat melts
under its own rafters
carved by flies

skull of a bird
the great geographies
drained to sutures,
stitched between flat bones

a suicide poet's skeleton lies
in hallowed ground
under a gravestone hard to find,
poorly kept, and sometimes
vandalised by literary tourists who tear
'Hughes' from the stone
leaving 'Sylvia' alone,
who can't have read *The Birthday Letters*

brooks toil in the valley to join
the hardest-worked river in England
only the rain never tires

Maths Questions

If all the people in the world
Faced west and began walking simultaneously
At about four miles an hour,
How much faster would the Earth spin on its axis?
And what would happen to national borders?
If all the people in the world
Did twenty minutes daily exercise on bicycles or treadmills
Attached to generators, would they
Produce enough electricity to power the planet?
If all the people in the world sang Middle C at the same time
What would it sound like? Especially
If they were all walking westward?
If all the people in the world simultaneously
Prayed to God (or whatever) and asked for peace,
How much peace would that produce,
And what units could be used to measure it?
If all the people in the world bought this poem for a penny,
Could I take early retirement and study higher mathematics?

For Professor Jonathan Sawday, June 2009

(on the occasion of his leaving the English Department at Strathclyde to take up a Chair at Saint Louis University in the USA)

It probably began as usual
not with shipwreck but an act of disobedience;
Crusoe went to sea and came to see
his fate as due to sin – defiance of the father;
is this an apt comparison –
can we think of Jonathan's career being somehow launched
by a forbidden trip to see The Who live at Leeds?
should we see him landing on the desert shore of this
    department,
nine years building a fortress,
tending goats, sorting wheat from chaff,
building a boat too heavy to drag to the waves,
saving us from cannibals:
did we save him, or he us?
or should we think Homer's Odysseus, that wily seadog
fought over by gods, carrying his crew from storm to storm
without map, compass or GPS,
wrecked on every island under the sun,
called by sirens, clubbing one-eyed father figures,
through indirections finding directions out,
carrying his scars in secret,
losing most of his crew in finding home:
have we lost him, or he us?
or perhaps he's Tennyson's Ulysses
striking out again for the open waters to the west,
Penelope at the helm,
breasting the tide of all those homecoming Scots,
dreaming of Ahab or Huck Finn on the Mississippi?

we stand here, remains of the clan on the harbour of tears,
looking westward with Norman McCaig
where 'the wrecked sun founders though its colours fly';
we turn to seek another skipper
– such another one who can take their rum as well as he,
hold fast to the helm in every weather,
lead us athwart the storm,
navigate the Gulf of Corryvreckan,
and leave us such another set of stories
in which the wind gets higher with every telling.

Moving from Glasgow to Blanefield, May 2010

A hundred Pickfords' flat-pack boxes waiting
To be unfolded, taped, filled, sealed. 4000 books to be packed.
Drawers of desks to be sorted. Folders to be unfolded.
Long-lost forgotten things turn up and tug the heart. That letter
In a box, even just the envelope with a foreign stamp, her
Handwritten version of my old address, open up strata of the past;
Fossils turn up in unexpected places, between
Books, tucked into old concert programmes that take me back;
Old tickets, scrapbooks, memories of the woman who bore me,
Photographs of her as a young girl yearning for a future
That was not to be, or at her sister's wedding arm in arm
With a handsome sailor, a lover perhaps whom she regretted
And settled for my father, just as I regret
Her loss and all the pain I could not relieve,
Either by being or doing. Packing my life
Into a hundred boxes involves unpacking, sifting and sorting,
Binning what I can and crying over what I can't avoid or change.
I thought I'd straightened my life into a linear story leading to here and now,
But in the process of moving from here to there I find the order I'd created
Was a shelter from the storm on shifting sands. And now I'm committed
To this moving business, this metaphor for opening up
Folds of memory that covered shards of grief and joy.
I'd forgotten that drawing, that unread diary,

That badge from a demonstration that was supposed to save
 the world.
All these fragments shored against my ruin, charged with
 memory and desire,
Dead weight which I must lug around on my back,
Snatches of songs half heard from the past.
Take that mirror …
But I no longer wish to propagate such reflections.
You moved in ten years ago in May
And we are moving out together in another May
To a house we fell in love with and fell in love
All over again. The first time I've moved with a woman,
The first woman who has moved with me.

Running out of Ink at Fifty-Seven

I've been writing since I began to scrawl;
in primary school, I recall,
I had a treasured fountain pen
with turquoise ink; if it wasn't for writing,
I wouldn't have no joy at all;

now I'm fifty-seven, writing
late into the night like writers
often do; last night
a window popped up telling me
my ink is running low; don't write
merely for the press, Coleridge said,
while doing precisely that.
He ran out of the shaping power and the joy –
nobody supplied them anymore:
Sara and William and Dorothy
all ran out on him.
But when I read his late love poetry,
his poetry of despair,
I still have a well of tears for one
who got me writing all those years ago.
Lines of loss and failure have a shaping power
that gives a sense of joy in agony
and lets me hear his scream in the storm.
There are streams of ink running
like granite intrusions into every crevice
of another glorious sunset.

For Doori: In Memoriam, 30 October 2010

Before I heard you'd died today
In your master's arms I was walking
Across Flanders Moss, late
Autumn sun almost flat out,
The Forth flooding its banks, thinking
I'd found a new walk for you,
An English Setter who lived with English settlers like me,
In a village not far from here;
But at that moment you were already
Dead or dying, the final injection releasing
Fatal fluid into your veins, easing
You from pain, humiliation;
I imagined taking you across the Moss in your prime,
Glimpsing you now and again as you ranged
Unbridled, far and wide, leaping long grass
Like a dolphin hurdling the waves
Just for the fun of it, crashing
Through woods; it seemed you would never tire
As you sprinted over moor and mountain
Yet biddable with call or whistle beyond the range
Of human ears; at that moment
When I remembered you as you were,
In the pride of your electric life,
I knew you were deaf, emaciated,
The nervous energy of your primal charge
Reduced merely to nerves;
If I could animate you again
Through apostrophe like this,
I'd hesitate:
Unless those coiled muscles
Could be pumped again with raw impulse,

That heart with wild blood,
It's best this way. You were trapped
By evolution and language,
But when you fixed me with that penetrating stare
You seemed to have a sense of selfhood more intense
Than we believe is possible for your kind,
An urge to communicate something more
Than you were deemed to know;
More alert than many human beings,
With knowledge of all the walks and trails
You'd blazed in the National Park like
Australian Aborigines map
The pathless deserts of their Dreamtime land.
I imagine you still running them.

A Conversation Poem at Nether Stowey, Summer 2011

I came with my pregnant wife
all the way from Scotland
to visit West Country places where
you and William and Dorothy became friends,
found lyrical ballads on the Quantocks,
ancestral voices in the combes,
ancient mariners around the harbours, talked
the visionary talk of youth and plotted
revolution in poetry. In the post-card village
that resented your residence and now
trades on your name, I stand
thwarted in the street, shut out
while English National Heritage,
an organ you would no doubt celebrate,
refurbishes the cottage where you launched,
with that pair of glorious siblings,
Romantic poetry in England.
I may have missed beauties and feelings
such as would have sweetened
the way I teach your poetry, but
I have also wandered in gladness
those hills and combes, guided
by your shaping imagination.

During your lifetime
I wouldn't have got a word in edgeways –
the muses were dumb while Apollo talked
a thousand things a minute and nightingales,
a great river sweeping away rocks, sweeping
poets off their feet. And though your voice

seems silent now, you may be stunned to know
you did not write in vain, that readers
through the living world still read the poems
you feared would rot with you in the grave,
which go on talking while there are ears to hear
and future generations.

But you'll never walk down Lime Street anymore,
or visualize your friends' excursions
from that lime-tree bower I'd hoped to see
where your garden borders on the orchard of your friend.

You died about the time that Darwin
sailed on the Beagle; and though
you asked his grandfather what did it matter
the age of the earth and how it was formed,
your defence of Christian mysteries through science
could not have stood the test of time
and evidence. There is grandeur
in the view of life that Darwin sees
in a tangled bank quite different
from the grandeur that you wove
from tangled impulses of a brain
evolved to survive the teeth and claws
of a nature you dared not imagine.

At Mary St Ottery your father's vicarage –
from where you were banished to the city,
pent mid cloisters dim – has been demolished;
a note in the tourist information office asks
how to make more of your fame. The Otter,
dear native brook you haunted as a child,
flows down to a coast that during your lifetime

began to yield fossils and bones of ages past,
vestiges of creatures who lived and died
a hundred million years before the birth of Christ,
when Britain lay under an ancient sea; at Lyme Regis
we walked the Cobb where Louisa Musgrove
fell in love in a novel you seem not to have read,
and the French lieutenant's woman
later looked out to sea, lashed
by winds and waves and the tongues
of the devout, and we played at being geologists
in the Blue Lias Jurassic cliffs –
mudstone, thin beds of limestone –
where giant skeletons were found by Mary Anning
braving landslides and winter storms:
ichthyosaurs, plesiosaurs, pterosaurs,
fossils of unknown fish, creatures not imagined
in your philosophy though you must have read the news;
we found fossils of ammonites, whose organic whorls
would have delighted you as emblems of poetic forms
shaped by imagination, yet actually made
by natural selection in a manner and a time
that awakens and overwhelms
imagination. Knowing all this,
knowing what you wouldn't have wanted
to know, we still read your poetry,
not as spontaneous overflows
of transcendental imagination,
wisdom of the sage of Highgate,
but as vestiges of the creative struggles
of the most brilliant spirit of the age to shape
a poetry to match his needs and theories
which yet reveals your fears in solitude,
dejection, intimations of mortality,

fears that even a soul like Milton's
can know death, that the creed of nature
you shared with William might be creative
self-delusion, that constancy
to ideal love may be constancy
to self-projected images – sustaining
fictions against the loss of all
that seems to make life meaningful,
poems more important
than all the schools of criticism
that now dissect your work,
some of which you founded.

That is why I stand outside your cottage,
pursuing these holiday meditations,
despite the fear of Thomas Hardy,
a poet born soon after your death,
that dead poets might reprove those literary tourists
who visit their hoary houses.

Your voice crosses the silent void
of two centuries; you make me speak in a form
that you created, a conversation that will end
not when the speakers are mere dust,
or when the frail shells of books,
the magnetic patterns of digital memories,
give way to as-yet unimagined means
for storing creations of human minds,
but when the planet itself has engulfed
rocks and stones and trees and human kind
in its never-ending geostrophic cycle.
When we are mere matter
folded into the strata of the future,

vestiges of ourselves and our creations,
there will be no evolved creatures looking
for our skeletons and fossils emerging
from cliff-faces on empty shores,
no English National Heritage,
no writing of poetry, no wedding guests
listening spellbound to ancient mariners' tales.
Only then will your conversation finally yield
to silence.

A Penny Drops

A penny drops
with a familiar ring
I can't quite place,
a clink of copper on stone,
runs in a wide arc
on smooth rim across
smooth floor, slows
into a tight turn, hula hoops
with a crescendo of cymbals
into its resting place, head up
and proud, hiding crowned portcullis
with chains; a coin of the realm
very like the farthings I loved as a boy
but worth much less and not worth
stooping for – you can't spend
a penny today, it's a token pledge;
its value drops by the minute;
since 1992 they've been magnetic,
minted in copper-plated steel,
but don't attract their kind.

Yet when it dropped like that
I recalled those farthings,
realised their worth,
given by parents and grandparents
for chores done fifty years ago and more;
just a fourthling of an old penny
(tenth of a new), but each
could buy a sweet from jars
in the village shop, now closed;
they had wrens on their tails,

kings and queens on their heads;
they could be stored
in a money box I made at school,
dove-tail joints and all,
and have stayed by me
while those who gave them
have gone to the grave;
no longer legal tender
I tender them more dearly
for those dear ones
whose lives are spent.

Nothing we save can save us,
not even treasured souvenirs.
That penny on the floor
means nothing to me now,
though on second thoughts
I'll stoop to gather it
for the child in my wife's womb
coming so late into my life
and all the more precious for that;
I'll add it to my hoard of copper wrens
for him or her to value when I'm gone.
It's worth looking after the pennies.

A Ming Imperial Porcelain Flask

(The Burrell Collection, Glasgow, April 2014)

In the deepest deeps of old slow time,
Five thousand miles from here,
Two continents of clay collide,
Two halves of China merge between
The Yellow and the Yangtze.

Twenty thousand years ago
Potters working in a cave
Formed and fired the southern clay,
Made pots in Jiangxi province:
Shards and bones remain.

In the Xuande reign of the Great Ming,
Six hundred years ago,
A peasant took a bamboo spade
And dug in beds of clay.

Women mixed the kaolin
With pottery stone and quartz,
Water from a mountain stream
And feldspar from the earth.

A potter took the earthen clay
And made a wonder with his hands,
A flask half a metre high,
Thin as eggshell, light as air.

Standing empty in silent halls
More than half a thousand years,
Dynasties rose and disappeared;
Civil wars and revolutions

Destroyed the world that made it;
On a slow boat from China's shores,
Fifty years and more ago,
It came to the heart of an empire

Whose sun was finally setting;
Stood empty in the echoing halls
Of cabinets and galleries;
Now it stands before us here.

Cobalt lotus leaves and tendrils
Stretch around its silent form,
Never living, never dying,
Ice-blue blossoms will not fade.

Frozen there six hundred years
By fired transparent glaze,
Never will *lian* be bare, [this lotus; 蓮]
It cannot shed its leaves.

A beautiful porcelain flask reveals
A truth that's not so beautiful,
That all who gaze upon *chan zhi* [decorative foliage on
Will not outlive this piece of clay. the flask; 纏枝]

A Quiet Revolution in Blanefield, 18 September 2014

Beech leaves spiral in a gentle wind,
Trickle along the pavement,
Gather at street corners,
Hardly making a sound.

A season turns
On a quiet morning,
Half-a-dozen men and women,
Retired, reticent,
Greet me as I stroll
Undecidedly
To Edmonstone Hall,
Legacy of the local laird.

A poster on a notice board
Says neither yes nor no
But 'A Village Remembers' –
A book that tells the stories
Of the men whose names are carved
In stone
On the war memorial across the road,
Just like the one in the English hamlet
Where I was born,
Whose crumbling sandstone
Only half erased
The names of several men
Whose surname was my own,
Whose stories were unknown to me.

I think about my son,
Born three years ago in Glasgow,
English father, Chinese mother,
He has no choice,
No need to choose.

Standing in the booth,
Pencil poised,
Faced with a question
That seems clear enough,
I find I cannot think it through
After a life of thought.

A cross is made,
The paper folded,
Slipped into a box.
No exit polls, no chanting crowds,
No policeman on the street,
Just a few quiet men all going grey
Sharing stories of the past.

Making my way home,
My little plot of Scotland,
I notice all the Saltires saying yes.
I'm tempted
To take the water pipe road
Towards Dumgoyne,
But this poem has begun
To nudge into my mind.

If anything, the breeze
Is dying down, the leaves
Await an impulse
That might never come again.

We've had the driest, warmest, stillest
September since records first began,
Reawakening roses and thistles,
But tomorrow will come
By the turning of the world,
Gravity holding
Even the lightest leaves
In their place, unmoved only
To the casual eye.

An overnight storm
Could strip those trees
And fill these streets
With quickening leaves,
And turn the world,
For better or for worse,
Upside down and inside out.

Let it be.

Souvenirs of Ivka

So much was left unsaid, undone, between us
when we parted on that urban autumn day
forty years ago; your father
taking his family back
to the Yugoslavia of his youth
couldn't imagine his daughter
loving outside the bounds
and bonds of his tradition.

You gave me *Poems of the Late T'ang*
and quoted Thoreau on the title page –
'All I can do for my friend
is be his friend' – but you signed
'with love'. After the first poem –
Tu Fu's 'Autumn Meditation' –
'Gems of dew wilt and wound the maple trees
In the wood' – you added lines of your own:
'There's a yellow leaf on the pavement,
just fallen, still full of summer'; you slipped
that leaf between the leaves;
it's still intact, beautiful in death
and full of memories.

We shared a passion every Monday evening
in a college classroom
for tales of young love's agonies,
for Lawrence's *Rainbow*
and Shakespeare's *Troilus*;
you worked in Northampton Public Library
where we often met; you left
a disused library card

in that book of Chinese poems –
David Campbell's *The Ephemeral Islands*:
'A natural history of the Bahamas …
providing insight into changes that have taken place'.
On the back you translated a sentence from Lawrence
into your mother tongue: I still don't know
what it means or what you meant
to me or I to you.

I gaze at wounded autumn trees
still full of summer,
recall our last chaste kiss, and hope
that you survived the war
that tore apart your father's country.

I Live on Grass

I live on grass,
Stand, walk, run, kneel,
Lie and feed on grass;
Spend my days with bowed head
Gazing and grazing
On grass;
You live on my weaned lambs,
And eventually me,
My butchered limbs;
You only eat grazers;
Fellow carnivores you hunt for fun
Or seek to save;
Foxes prey on us: you chase them down
With dogs, like dogs,
Or try to ban the hunt;
Another breed of dogs,
Bred by you, herd us
Like wolves who single out
The young and weak and lame;
You are top dogs in the pack,
The pact of carnivores.

My Euphonium

(for J. Simon van der Walt, 13 June 2018)

I call you my euphonium,
you sound real good to me;
so I'm writing this encomium,
these words of eulogy.

You came into my life at puberty,
I've loved and hated you since then;
we never will be free of one another,
we'll never want to be.

Making music through the night,
muted jazz at the midnight hour,
post-romantic melodies at dawn,
you always know the key I'm in.

Busking in Buchanan Street,
we played real good but not for free,
made music and money in the rush-hour rain;
stopped the town with real good sounds.

You stand on your own on the stage,
pipes and valves exposed to the world,
precision engineering like an old steam train,
or one of those buildings whose inside

is on the outside, postmodern and polished,
or like some intricate organism under the sea,
or Celtic knots on a standing stone.
But you only sing in my arms,

cradled like a baby or my only love,
lips to lips and breath to breath,
a thing of beauty, to me at least.
I'm willing to admit the fact

you sound more like an elephant
than ascending larks at dawn,
no heart soars to hear your song but mine,
and yet you make them laugh.

Lie here on my knees, I'll rest my arms on you,
cradle my chin, count the bars,
bring you back to my lips
for a last extended intimate kiss.

I call you my euphonium,
you sound real good to me.

Childcare in Fosters Booth

when I was a boy in primary school
my mother worked as a dress-maker in the town
to add to my father's labourer's pay
and get out of the house, I guess;
I don't know who minded my brothers
but I often stayed with my Nan and Pap
in Fosters Booth, where long ago a forester
built his wooden hut; they rented
a tiny house, two up, two down,
an outside unflushed loo (wooden board,
round hole, smelly drop), a zinc bath
in front of the fire which heated water
in kettles on the black-leaded range,
a house where I spent the first year of my life
with dad and mum in the cold back room,
now filled with dank papers, magazines and dust,
and a room at the top of the wooden hill,
creaking bare wooden stairs, where
Pap now stored his winter vegetables
in dry earth; some days I helped
in his allotment, he warned me
away from the cesspit – an unfenced pond
of slurry drained from a cattle-shed in which
he said I'd drown and never be found;
washday in the washhouse was women's work
but I liked to help – water was heated
in a huge copper boiler by burning
wood and coal in a fireplace beneath;
clothes were ladled with a large copper bell
with holes and a long wooden handle, plunging
up and down; a mangle turned

by an eager boy squeezed
water from cloth; baskets
of heavy wet clothes were heaved
up mopped concrete steps,
hung on a line in a shared backyard;
on Sundays I'd walk with Pap
along the Watling Street,
the Roman road that passed
just feet from the door and headed north,
finding empty matchboxes
for one of my collections
with pictures of heroes, like Amy Johnson
in her flying cap, on covers;
he was taciturn, which suited me, but
we sometimes talked of setting snares
and I'd watch him cobble his own shoes, cutting leather
that smelt of work and craft and care,
better than the Woodbines that never left his lips;
in season, Nan and I picked mushrooms
on misty mornings in a wondrous field, fried-up dozens
and sold the rest to the pub down the road
where she'd have a glass of stout in the lounge
that smelt of adulthood;
but mostly I remember long afternoons
when they would doze and I would read
cartoon strips in piles of Daily Mirrors –
Garth, who battled villains across the world
and travelled through time; Andy Capp
with a fag glued to his mouth,
half-drunk pint on the bar;
my favourite was 'The Perishers' –
a smart young orphan boy called Wellington
and Boot, his crazy Old English Sheepdog,

who lived at first in a concrete pipe
and then moved up in the world to an unused
railway station, selling trucks to gormless Marlon
boosted with go-faster stripes.
No one seemed to care for them but me.
I stood for hours at the window, watching
occasional cars go by on the Roman road;
there were blebs in the glass – bubbles
of air that bent the outside world,
and made it wobble when I moved.
A clock ticked away the seconds of my life;
a sepia face of my mother's sister Joyce,
who died when young of Polio,
haunted me then and haunts me still.
These are my memories of childcare
with my Nan and Pap,
seen through blebs in my mind.

On Inchcolm

Standing here on an Inch of the Forth,
Here on the rocks of ages,
Where hermits, saints and monks have stood
A thousand years and more,
Singing praises of this place
To sound of timbrels,
Harps, trumpets and strings,
High-sounding cymbals of joy,
And the Little Dunkeld Bell,
Singing to the ghosts
That haunt these stones and crumbling walls,
Remembering deeds of the dead,
Buried in earth, walled up in walls,
Walls of worship, defence of the land,
Conjuring all their yesterdays
And tomorrows yet to come,
Past, present, future, here and now,
Voices summoned by bells,
Versicle and response.

Celebrated islander, hope of Scots,
Exiled fox or dove,
This place is dedicated to you;
Your loud, melodious voice
Heard on the hills,
Commanded once the winds,
Drew water from a rock;
Go to your rest,
Go the way of your fathers,
When the bell strikes in the middle of this night.

Buildings raised to the sky are standing still
In ruins that lift the soul,
An island clothed with beauty and with strength
Repels all enemies;
These walls have ears and eyes,
Have witnessed
Birds of the air and whales in the Forth,
Endless cycles of the earth,
Sun and moon and stars of heaven,
Winter and summer, days and nights,
Ice and snow, shower and dew.

Let us sing from memory in the flickering dark,
The last light of a winter's eve
On mountains and hills of the north,
Turn to face the east and then the west,
Holding twenty candles for unending night,
Brief candles for a long-gone saint
Morning and evening star,
Light from east and west.

Let us sing of this place in the choir
Stretching and bending the notes,
Sing as the sun sinks in the west,
Stained-glass shards of red and gold
Scattered on darkening hills,
Keep watch for break of day,
To lay its light on these walls and us.

The wind is still from the east,
The deep is calm,
The flood lifts up its waves and seems to speak,
Voice of many waters,
And the Little Dunkeld Bell.

Self-Examination at 63

Chronic sinusitis in my head, no cure
Apparently; tinnitus in my ears,
Seventies' rock still echoing down the years;
Some molars have gone – I thought the implants
Would be trouble-free and last forever
But lymph glands in the neck
Sometimes swell; acupuncture cured
My asthma thirty years ago,
But hasn't worked on anything since;
Friendly bacteria pacify
Irritable bowel every month or so;
Diverticular disease is not a disease,
My GP says, but a condition that can't be cured
And could become a painful 'itis';
My bladder is retentive, urine
No longer flows like a mountain burn –
Though frequent, urgent peeing
Is common in men my age,
That's no comfort; back spasms every year or so
Bring days of agony and therapy;
These hips have supported me and heavy packs
Up and down a hundred mountains and more
And one at least is bearing the cost;
A knee gives way on stairs and hills; a bunion?
Well these feet have carried me and all my burdens
All these years; hardly worth mentioning
The fungal infection in both toenails
That's survived everything the NHS has thrown at it
These last ten years.

Not all in the mind
And the GPs are kind,
And though it's absurd
It might turn on a word:

Illness? Disease? Condition?
Minor ailments, my GP said,
Trying to help,
And none of them will leave me dead.

He's right, of course, but none
Can be healed or cured
And each one clamours for attention
In its turn,
And new ones come on thick and fast;
Death by a thousand cuts is worse
Than one clean blow, death in life;
That which does not kill us,
Does not make us stronger.

Add to these the never-ending
Creations of a working brain – excessive
Health anxiety's the latest medical term –
That rise in some untrodden region of my mind
Beyond the reach of therapy, fatal ailments
Every one, a thousand deaths,
Which melt into air when scanned,
Troubling visions of a beating mind.

It's all just growing old, of course,
I need to be resigned,
I cannot change reality,
And I cannot change my mind.

The Name Business

I'm here today
asking for an investment
of £100,000
for ten percent of a company called
The Name Business.
In today's competitive world
small businesses need distinctive images.
My company supplies creative names
to shops and other enterprises
to help them market themselves
as stand-out brands. I have a degree
in English literature and write poetry.
My skill in verbal art and desire
to help companies grow, partnered
with your expertise, money and contacts
will help The Name Business
achieve a huge profit in the next three years
and improve the poetry of shopping.
Thank you for listening. I'm happy to answer your questions.
Some examples of names and contracts already achieved?
'The Definite Article' – an arts magazine I helped to found.
My first ever shop name was 'Fleece' –
An expensive up-market knitwear shop
owned by parents of friends: not used.
'Curry Out' for an Indian takeaway –
not yet offered to any client.
Most recently I thought of a great name
for a slimming club: 'Slim Chance'!
My wife and business partner didn't like the pun
but I might approach some local clubs.
I even thought of a name

for a business that doesn't yet exist:
'Complimentary Medicine': clients
pay to receive compliments
that make them feel better about themselves.
How about 'On-Line Delivery'
for a monger selling rod-caught fish on the internet –
or 'Something Fishy' if that's too obscure?
Market research? On the bus
on the way to work I scan shop signs.
It's depressing and hilarious and full
of opportunities. Turnover?
Good name for a pastry company!
All Out? A gay cricket club?
You won't be investing?
I'm not at all surprised. Whoever
thought of the name anyway? Whoever
heard of dragons giving away the gold in their dens
to the questing hero?

The Old Jokes Make Us Laugh

The old jokes make us laugh,
The old songs make us cry,
Old folks make us realise
We didn't drop from the sky.

The only news is old news,
Nothing new under the sun,
Old friends help us realise
The past will never be done.

Olden days were golden days,
In some ways that is true,
The older we wax the wiser we wane,
No longer shocked by the new.

The past is another country,
Where it's impossible to live,
The future is a Neverland,
The present is all we can give.

What Happens to a Bee with Hay Fever?

What happens to a bee with hay fever,
To a fish afraid of water,
An eagle of heights,
A tree whose bark is worse than its bite?

Whereas the leaves and leavings
Of human beings have been gathered into vaults
Just under the surface of the planet,
Prevented from mingling with the mould
Of millions of years of living-dying things,
Storing ten thousand years of human cultures,
Leaves and spent lives of plants and animals
And all our pre-historic ancestors
Have added their lot to enrich the soils formed
Of the debris of mountains worn and washed away
By relentless waters of the world over billions of years.
None of this is noticed by the creatures who give their all.
It is we, for good or ill, who gather and share
Observations, hunt species for food, trophies, specimens
In vaults and sacred causes, we
Who spoil and nurture soil, paint sunlit hills,
Trace geostrophic cycles and oceanic currents, thrill
To whale-songs and mingle our poems and twitterings
In glorious banal cacophony, cross-currents,
Culture. There are no bees with hay fever, only
In human imaginations struck by a thought
In the middle of a summer night, but
Bees are disappearing, sick with something
That we perhaps created, exhausted perhaps
By thousands of years of pollinating the crops that feed

Billions of specimens of a species that keeps them and their
 honey.
There are no fish out of water except on mongers' slabs,
And fewer now in water than ever before. There are trees
Whose bark absorbs our exhalations, whose leaves
Supply our oxygen, whose wood becomes
And heats our houses. Consider the rain that washes
The air we breathe, waters food we eat, makes up
The bulk of our bodies.

Hospital or Death?

'Which do you want – hospital or death?' My father
would ask, holding up one large fist
and then the other. Aged 10, I took him seriously:
in his forties his biceps bulked large in my eyes. He'd
spent a lifetime working on farms; laying
hedges was his trade: cutting saplings
half-way through with a bill-hook, bending
and weaving them to make a living fence
like basket-making. In the spring
he would bring back the blown eggs of rare hedgerow birds
telling me their names,
and I would carefully lay them labelled
in boxes of sawdust. His muscles were honed, too,
by chopping wood with an axe for the fire, digging
garden and allotment, lifting spuds with a fork, heaving
sack-loads of this and barrowloads of that.
He'd been in Africa and Italy in the war
and learned to swim on the beaches of Palestine
as Britain carved out a state for the Jews;
there are photos of him in shorts,
a boy from a farming village in Northamptonshire, looking
brown and fit and confident, belying the trauma of war
that might help explain how a father could offer such a choice
to his first-born only half in jest;
how a father could work the garden with a son,
gathering the fruit of earth and toil, and suddenly rage
if he dropped the sack or broke the eggs; how
he would later fall apart in body and soul as age
and illness, loneliness and poverty repaid
a lifetime of work in the fields and factories and wars
   of England.

Biceps atrophied, lungs shot by nicotine, humiliated by
    state care,
he lost control of bladder and bowels
and lost control of his life. Towards the end,
out of nowhere, he told us his battalion
had been chosen to be among the first troops
to march into liberated Rome flanked by cheering crowds.
Hospital or death? None of us get to choose
in the end.

First Apostrophe to an Invisible Embryonic Being, 16 August 2011

I thought that I would open up a dialogue
That we'll keep going for as long
As we'll have together on this earth,
My hand resting on your mother's
Extending belly, membrane between
Our parallel worlds, sounding board
And drum-skin for two-way signals,
Punch-bag for your martial arts. We think
You're twenty-three weeks old,
Based on measurements from crown to coccyx;
We're vague about the moment of conception –
We never knew that you'd set out
On your journey towards our lives
Until ten weeks ago. It's true
I had a premonition when your grandmother
Left on her long journey back to Malaysia –
You must have been a tiny bundle
Of undetected replicating cells at the time –
When I strangely felt it's just the three of us again:
How could one leaving three leave three?
It's four weeks now since you began
Your aqua-natal classes,
Wild swimming in dark amniotic seas.
Although you won't be coming out here for months
We've already seen you – ultrasound technology
Has probed your inner world: sounds
Beyond the range of human hearing,
An echo system like bats use
To navigate their way through darkness
Not unlike yours, became electrical pulses,
Became images on a screen
Printed in black and white –

The first photos of you, glimpses
Of another world, blurred and grainy,
Like first astronauts on the moon
Forty years ago, beamed around the world.
At thirteen weeks you were meditating,
Staring into inner darkness,
Calmly getting to know yourself,
Unaware that we were spying on you;
At twenty weeks you'd grown, of course,
Grown restless and wrestling
Invisible opponents, resisting
The midwife's probing for anomalies.
I don't know why I'm explaining all this now –
There'll be world enough and time, I hope.
But more than ever I want to seize the days
That mark your progress towards the outside world
And all the things I want to share with you. Above all
I want to see you lying full of life
Upon your mother's breast, to feel the soft soles
Of feet that will need to harden if they are
To tread this earth. We know you hear sounds
From inner space and outer world:
Do you dance to the beat of your mother's heart?
Do you know your father's voice?
If I spoke these lines out loud perhaps
You'd understand the tone if not the words,
The rhythms though not the metaphors.
And if you can't yet join this dialogue, add
Words from depths of the womb
To the first poem that I write for you,
Know your very being speaks to me
In ways I never imagined.

Expecting (13 December 2011)

Rain beats roof above our heads
like all the grain from the world's plains
tumbling endlessly from a hopper,
all the waters of the Atlantic caught up
in the world's hydrologic cycle
breaking on our slates
then running with the flood
that pours into the burn at the bottom of our road;
all this water plunging
towards the point of freezing; atoms
have almost given up moving
and the earth would break a spade;
the four winds strive to land a storm
of body-blows on this house, bending
overhanging trees like longbows ready to fire
storm-tipped arrows;
a sky robbed of light by clouds
pregnant with the deluge;
the sun's abandoned this northern land
and headed south;
we huddle in our loft like emperor penguins
guarding eggs at the South Pole, expecting
contractions that signal the first coming
of a new being navigating
the pelvic canal and the curve of Carus
towards this waiting world, bringing
warmth and light, release
of pent-up waters, a flowing
of milk and honey, a promise
of spring not far behind.

Snow Baby

First light of the day, first snow of the year
swaddles the hills, wraps the trees,
blankets our drive; first hesitant steps
print a pathway to our door
delivering mail; first cry
of rooks in the trees heralds
the hunt for food; and you
make your first kicks of the day
against the swaddling womb,
levering yourself, readying yourself –
whether we're ready or not –
to make your first appearance
on the scene of this world, first cry,
first day of your outer life (you'll always be
nine months' older than your age),
first day of our new life. We've waited
long for you, wondered who you are
and who you will become; we've prepared
what we can, rehearsed and read and been
to ante-natal classes; but now we're timing
the intervals between contractions
and your needs have taken possession
of your mother's body and there's a tinge of terror
in our delight, visions of a midnight
expedition through arctic snow, breaking
waters, labour pains, navigation
without the help of GPS,
delivering you and mother-to-be
into the hands of midwives trained
to deliver you to the snowbound world.

Walking with You in the Babybjörn at Eight Months Old

Your back rests against my chest,
We face the world together;
Mostly, we're quiet,
Hardly say a word, hunters
Ranging the forest, watching,
Looking, staring, listening:
Burns and streams and rivers,
Sheep and dogs and Highland cows,
Swallows sweeping the air,
Buzzards surfing the wind, mountains
On the northern edge of the world, moss
On craggy ash-tree bark, horses
Galloping in the fields about, wind
Made visible in sun-lit leaves,
Grandfather's tartan green umbrella keeps
Off rain and shine and twirls above your head,
The burn flowing beside our road and under
The bridge where we stand: we never see
The same stream twice and yet it's always the same –
'Water, water' pouring out of the hills, flowing
Into the Blane and through your dreams,
The first river on earth for you;
Every dog rivets your attention;
Crows fly overhead for you as crows fly,
Scoring circles on the sky; old horses,
Heads bowed to the earth, feeding
On meagre grass amongst patches of mud,
Are wondrous; you stare for spellbound minutes
At ever-changing shapes and lights, listen
To forever-changing sounds; horses

And streams and trees share the sources
Of the power that courses through
Your body's electric streams;
Flying manes in mountain winds
Take your breath away,
Everything new under the sun striking
And stroking your eyes, ears, skin, mouth:
Oh, brave new world
That has such a creature in it.

Hydrocortisone Behind my Knees

Hydrocortisone behind my knees
And under my arms, twice a day,
Timodine in the crook of my neck
And around my genitals;
At every nappy change,
Sudocream for the red rash
Lurking in the folds of my skin;
Double Base four times every day
On back and front and arms and legs,
Epaderm for my cradle cap
Every other day;
And Oilatum for my bath sometimes,
Which does not spoil my fun.

Creams and ointments prescribed
For my own good, they say, but I
Fight them every time, scream and shout
Despite the songs and loving care
That come with them. Redness, itching,
Scratching dryness, crusting, flaking,
It just goes on and on… and I boil over.
That's what eczema means – look up the Greek.

Cooling Fire

Aidan means the fiery one;
Shan-Yang, spreading benevolence
And heat; Furniss sounds
Like a hot fiery oven; eczema:
To boil over; born in the heart of winter,
On Christmas Eve, you melted hearts,
Lit an everlasting fire;
But your internal fire inflames
Your skin; the story
Told by DNA can't yet be written differently;
But I can't accept this etymology,
Such definitions; and I have ways
To tell a different tale:
When you scratch and scratch and scratch
In the watches of the night
I lull you to sleep
With the sound of western oceans
Breaking on western shores,
Waters where dolphins play,
North-western winds whistle
Through machair; the songs
I sing are northern songs
That rang around the world
Fifty years ago and go on ringing still;
I tell of lonely fishermen
Who suffer salt spray on the longest
Coldest night of the year; my heroes
Struggle against polar winds and wonder
At Northern Lights, cool fires
That seem to burn the atmosphere
But shower the Earth with solar particles

That fall like snow; your generation
Will face realities of global warming, but
There is yet cold enough in the poles
To take you off the boil.
Jubilee beacons burn on wind-swept hills, their heat
Carried up to the highest, coldest
Layers of Earth's atmosphere
And then beyond the pull of gravity,
Beyond the outer planets, towards
The joy of absolute zero.
These cold stories battle the heat
Of DNA and definitions.

Driving to the Montessori Nursery in Killearn, July 2014

In the mornings we wait while the red light shows:
There are diggers and dumpers and men in hard hats,
Digging a hole in the road;
It seems this hole has always been crawling
Slowly through Killearn.

The light turns green and it's go, go, go:
On past the digger clawing stone from the hole,
Orange light flashing from the roof of its cab,
On past the dumper being filled up with rocks,
On past the saw that slices the road
In parallel lines that never will meet;
On past the men heaving shovels and picks,
Driving dumpers and diggers like heroes,
Haloed in glory for you.

In the evenings we wait for red to turn green,
But the diggers are silent and the dumpers
Are still; the men have gone to their dinners
We say, after toiling in heat the whole of the day;
They've been there all our yesterdays,
And'll be back on the job tomorrow.

Time is not a journey for you,
The here and now are forever,
Things are just the way they ought to be,
The way they simply are;
Daddy will always be daddy for you,
Driving this car along these roads;
Mummy's breasts will always run with milk

Like the river running past our door;
Life will always ping pong between
Nursery and home.

In the mornings we'll wait while the red light shows;
There'll be diggers and dumpers and men in hard hats,
Digging a hole in the road;
Evenings we'll wait for red to turn green,
Though the diggers are silent and the dumpers are still,
And the men have gone home to their glory.

A Sawing Horse

(In memory of Mr Webster, who taught me woodwork and technical drawing at Towcester Secondary Modern School in the 1960s.)

I made a sawing horse today,
a calm crisp February day
in my back garden, found
or formed the blueprint
in my mind and fashioned
wood and screws from B&Q
with handsaw, power drill, pencil,
try-square, measure, home-made
trestle, G-clamps, tools I learned to use
in Mr Webster's woodwork classes
fifty years ago,
a man of seasoned wood
of heart and grain, strong and flexible,
who taught the good old joints,
dovetail, mortice, tenon, secured
with pungent steaming collagen glue
made from horses' bones and hooves;
taught boys to work with aromatic woods –
teak, walnut, oak, mahogany,
cherry, ash and box –
with chisels, planes, saws and lathes,
sanded and polished with elbow grease,
carnauba wax, French polish;
taught skills and sayings
that come to me whenever I set to work:
'thumb-one-three' when holding tools,
'stand like a boxer' using a saw,

'make your cut on the waste side of the line' –
'loosely tighten' all your screws at first,
old saws perhaps, but they seemed
original wisdom to me,
still shape the way I work and teach my son;
six lengths of 4 by 2, imperial,
formed three St Andrews crosses
standing upright in a row,
off-centred, unequally spaced,
four horizontal battens, 3 by 1;
I made the horse for Aidan,
my six-year-old, who takes me
gathering wood in the forest
which he cuts and chops into logs
for the cast-iron fire-pit he wanted
for his latest birthday on Christmas Eve;
the horse holds logs for the saw and links
generations across time:
the design came from memory
of one my father had and let me use
when I was a boy cutting firewood
for the only fire we had
in that cold Cold Higham council house;
he showed me how to gather the logs
in a warm embrace, told me
that they warm us twice – when we saw them,
when they're burned, and I remember
the pride of working, helping out,
and I wonder now about that horse,
that form I called up in my mind
and copied today, taken for granted then
as a thing that simply was in the world,
wonder if he built it himself

and whether he felt what I feel today
at a handy job well done,
wonder how he knew the form –
perhaps his own father,
who lived a village away,
laboured on farms, built
his house, gathered wood, made
a horse like that; I seemed
to break the line, moving away,
teaching English, writing such stuff,
but lines must be cut
and joined and polished and keep
true to the grain, and books
are made of wood after all,
pulped in paper mills, cut to shape,
printed, pressed, sewed and glued;
a craft that binds words and wood
across lands and time and changed
the world; and teaching
is a kind of making, drawing out
what's in the wood – that was
Mr Webster's way,
and the things I made all those years ago
stay with me still, the joints still hold –
and the grain runs true
in every cell of Aidan's DNA,
whose need to build, saw, lop,
whittle, dig, rake from three years old
could not be thwarted;
and now I have time on my hands
I walk with him and help him find
the wood he seeks and self he wants to be,
and teach him what I learned of wood and soil

from teachers way back when;
I wonder why it's called a horse –
some have four legs, mine has six,
sticks up at both ends, head and tail,
uncomfortable to ride – I love
those old mysterious man-made
words and man-made things
and old-time man-made joints
holding them together time out of mind,
the poetry-making they make possible,
shaping the grain of being and time,
the shaping of wood by tools
that fit and shape the hand,
and mindfulness that comes
in the making; I could have bought
a horse from Amazon,
but money can't buy what we make
cannot make us what we want
to be.

*

Acknowledgements

'The Chameleon' was first published *The Definite Article* (1980) and in *Play for Three Hands* (1981).

'A Sepia Face' was first published in *The Definite Article* (1983).

'Crustacea', 'Break of Day', 'Corrosion', 'The Ceremony', 'Love Lyric', 'A Coefficient of Friction' and 'Study in Black and White' were first published in *Play for Three Hands* (1981).

'Despedida Federico Lorca' was first published in *Poesis* (1981).

'A Ming Imperial Porcelain Flask' was set to music by Eddie McGuire and performed by Harmony Ensemble at the Burrell Collection, Glasgow (12 April 2014), and at the British Museum (28 July 2014).

'On Inchcolm' was set to music by Eddie McGuire and performed by The Inchcolm New Music Ensemble of Heriot Watt University in Iona Abbey (30 June 2017) and in St Giles Cathedral, Edinburgh (1 July 2017).

www.ingramcontent.com/pod-product-compliance
Lightning Source LLC
Chambersburg PA
CBHW060401080526
44583CB00012B/422